Just "Plane" Haiku

Una Belle Townsend

Ubee Press

Yukon, OK 73099

ISBN: Hardback: 979-8-9869921-0-5 (hc)   Softback: 979-8-9869921-1-2 (sc)

Just "Plane" Haiku /Una Belle Townsend
1. Planes— poetry 2. Children's poetry 3. Haiku 4. Aviation 5. Airplanes 6. Planes--old and new
7. Glossary 8. Fun Facts 9. Photographs: Chris Townsend, Virgil Townsend, and Una Belle Townsend

811   Library of Congress Control Number: 2023940193

Ubee Press

Yukon, OK 73099

Dedication

Dedicated to my husband, Virgil, and to our two sons, Chris and Brian. You are all great pilots, and I appreciate your help with this book.

To Andrea Foster: Thank you for being my mentor, for your edits, your publishing skills, and your friendship.

Also, to all pilots who love to fly "in the wild, blue yonder." May you always fly safely, and return home to your loved ones.

Haiku

Haiku has three lines of 5, 7, 5 syllables.
It's usually about nature.
It has no title, but can have punctuation.
Haiku doesn't rhyme.
It creates a "snapshot" or an "in the moment memory."

Here is a haiku:

Haiku has three lines	5
Five, seven, five syllables	7
A Japanese poem	5

Many use a thesaurus or dictionary to find the exact synonym they need when writing their own haiku.

Good morning, sunshine
You have brightened up the world
With your big "Hello"

Beautiful sunrise
Climbing toward the hand of God
At peace with the world

Hello, Bonanza
Exciting flight planned today
Ready for take-off

A P-51
On display at an air show
"Hi ya Doc" on side

. . . . .

Beautiful redbird
Will enhance the cloudy sky
Like a Cardinal

On exhibition
Little plane, BD5J
Listens for comments

Cloudy day ahead
Pilot checking the weather
Might delay the flight

Sky Baby airplane
Held record as smallest plane
Over thirty years

Loops, spins, and spirals
Stunt pilot performs for crowds
Great day at air show

Aerobatic plane
Colorful bi-wing fuels up
Ready to perform

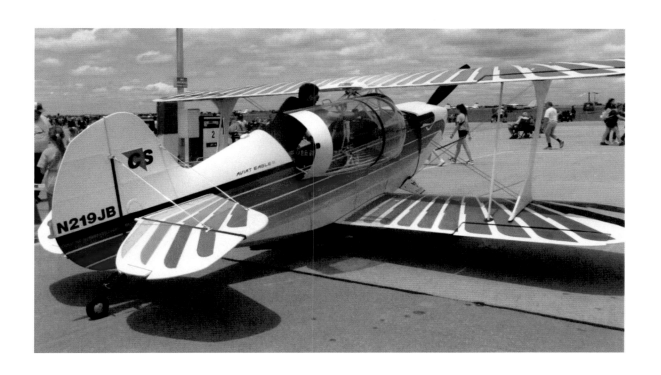

Playin' in the sky
Flippin' the plane upside down
Bustin' through the clouds

Shuttle on display
Visitors amazed at size
NASA proud of it

Space shuttle in flight
to Oklahoma City
Rides piggy-back style

Amphibious plane
Sitting alone on tarmac
Tied down and waiting

Seaplane approaches
Victoria vacation
Days of fun ahead

War plane on display
Veterans enjoy touring
Memories abound

Pilot cleans windshield
Of a huge B-17
Not an easy job

Facing enemy
Gunner in tight position
He must stay alert

Old warbird's gunner
B17 tail turret
Tiny position

Colorful biplane
Raptor's dark green fuselage
Showing scary teeth

A B-25
Sometimes called a PBJ
With ferocious beak

NavyS Blue Angels
Hanging in a huge museum
And still flying high

Blue Angels appear
Great skills displayed at air show
A big crowd pleaser

Crowd is excited
Navy's Blue Angels soar high
Formation flying

Super-sonic flight
Chuck Yeager in Bell X-1
Plane housed in museum

"Que Sera Sera"
First plane to land at South Pole
Now in Florida

Pilot in trouble
Control tower alerted
Help is on the way

A B-29
Only a few still flying
A retired bomber

Air Force One awaits
President and First Lady
Return to D.C.

Sleek looking King Air
Resting for a little while
And then homeward bound

A Navy pilot
Flying a T 28
Ready for take-off

Plane delayed hours
Pilot checking the weather
Sits and waits it out

Made in Switzerland
Patriotic PC12
Ready to fly high

Scary nose of plane
F-14 Tom Cat fighter
Housed inside hangar

Boomer, the guard dog
Pilots need to be aware
This dog means business

Unusual sky
Singed edges of vibrant clouds
Quivering heavens

Plane on carrier
Nicknamed "a stoof with a roof"
WF-1

Versatile airplane
Built to look for submarines
Now a Firebomber

Ercoupe on runway
Pilot waiting for clearance
Take-off should be soon

Derby Contestants
Weather delay, race on hold
Weather wins this time

Twilight and planes rest
Tomorrow is air derby
Who will win the race?

Night time approaching
Runway lights guide each pilot
For their safe return

End of the journey
Pilot ready for a rest
Finished for the day

Some Interesting Facts about the Planes

Page 11 - Home built planes—Many people like to build their own planes. They enjoy flying them and often go to fly-ins. Some use them as small work planes checking on their herds or on their land.

Page 17 - The Stits SA-2A Sky Baby is a single engine, single seat aircraft that was a homebuilt biplane. It held the record as smallest flown aircraft from 1952 to 1984.

Pages 19, 21, 23 - Aerobatic planes are sometimes called stunt planes. The pilots spin, roll, do spirals, sky write, or just have fun flying upside down.

Pages 25, 27 - On April 27, 1981, the Columbia shuttle landed at Tinker Air Force Base in Oklahoma City. It rode atop a B-747 and was on an overnight stopover following its first orbital mission. An estimated 200,000 people watched its arrival.

Pages 29, 31 - Amphibious planes land on water or land. Seaplanes take-off and land on water.

Page 33 - The Spirit of Freedom was a C-54 transport during the war. Afterwards, it participated in the Berlin Airlift. The Americans and British succeeded in delivering over 2.5 million tons of supplies to the City of Berlin to keep the people alive.

A Boxer dog named Vittles accompanied pilots, including his owner, and was credited with 130 missions. He had his own specially made parachute.

Page 35 - A B17 bomber made by Boeing. It was also called a "Flying Fortress."

Pages 37, 39 - The gunner on this B17 faced the enemy in a tiny, cramped position at the back of the plane.

Pages 45, 47, 49 - The Navy's Blue Angels fly in formation thrilling many crowds a year throughout the country. They delight thousands with their precision flying.

Page 51 - Chuck Yeager broke the sound barrier in a Bell X-1 experimental plane. The bright orange plane was named the "Glamorous Glynnis" in his wife's honor. It is housed at the National Air and Space Museum.

Page 53 - The first plane to land at the South Pole. It was named "Que Sera Sera." It was an R4D5L and also called DC3 or C47. It has a Day-Glo orange tail, and is housed at the National Museum of Naval Aviation at NAS Pensacola, FL.

Page 59 - Air Force One carries the President of the United States and others, including the First Lady, throughout the United States and to other countries.

Page 69 - This is an F-14 Tom Cat. It's a fighter plane.

Page 75 - An Airborne Early Warning Aircraft found on carriers was nicknamed "a stoof with a roof." WF-1

Page 77 - A post war P2V, the Neptune, was built by Lockheed. These planes were built to hunt submarines. After retirement from active duty some were converted to firebombers.

Simple Definitions

Aerobatic plane: A plane whose pilot performs rolls, may fly upside down, does spins, and sometimes, writes in the sky.

Airliners: Large planes which holds many passengers.

Amphibious Plane: A plane which can land on water or on land.

Aviator/Pilot: A person who has been trained to operate a plane.

Bi-wing: A plane which has two sets of wings.

Bombers: Planes whose main purpose is to bomb targets. Usually used in war situations.

Cargo: What the plane carries for a load.

Control Tower: A tower on the airport grounds that contains trained observers or controllers who advise pilots.

Flight plans: Pilots sometimes file flight plans before flying.

Formation flying: This takes place when several planes work together and fly together in a pattern or formation.

Gunner: A designated man who saw enemy planes and attempted to shoot at them from his position facing them in the back of the plane.

Passenger: A person who usually buys a ticket so that a pilot can fly him to a designated place.

Runway: A place for airplanes to take-off or land on an airfield.

Ramp or Tarmac: A place where planes sit before departing the airport or where they move to after landing.

Shuttle: A plane who carries astronauts into space for a designated time.

Skis: Some planes have skis so they can land on snow or ice.

Take-off: When a plane moves onto a runway area to begin the flight.

Warbirds: Planes used in wars which are usually retired when wars end. Some were transports which carried food and supplies, while others carried soldiers.

Una Belle Townsend is a retired teacher and librarian and the author of eleven published books. She graduated from East Texas Baptist College and acquired her Master's Degree at Stephen F. Austin State University. She received an Oklahoma Center for the Book Award, a Best in Juvenile Books Award from the Oklahoma Writer's Federation, Inc., an IRA/Children's Choice Award, and a Delta Kappa Gamma Women of Achievement in Poetry Award. She and her husband live in Yukon, OK.

Books by Una Belle Townsend

Grady's in the Silo
The Oklahoma Land Run
Racecar Driver's Night Before Christmas
The Great Elephant Escape
Sunsets and Haiku
Scanner
Clancy
Toby and the Secret Code
Scanner and the Icky Sticky Gum
Ben and the Missing Pony
Blazer's Taxi